Contents

Dumb dinosaurs? 4

Too dumb to fight 6

The great display 8

Inside the brain 10

Armoured stupidity 12

Bonehead 14

Fruit eater 16

Sunbathing 18

A second brain 20

Puppy brained 22

Brain fever 24

Desert walker 26

Dealing with fossils 28

Glossary 30

Find out more 31

Index 32

Some words are shown in bold, **like this**. You can find out what they mean by looking in the glossary.

Dumb dinosaurs?

When **dinosaurs** were first discovered, many people thought they must have been the dumbest animals to ever walk the Earth. But today, scientists think that some dinosaurs might have been quite clever. Most dinosaurs were smarter than crocodiles!

Some dinosaurs had a huge body, but a very small brain. They were probably dumber than other dinosaurs. However, we might never know how clever or dumb dinosaurs really were.

EXTREME DINOSAURS

WORLD's DUMBEST DINOSAURS

Rupert Matthews

www.raintreepublishers.co.uk
Visit our website to find out more information about Raintree books.

To order:
☎ Phone 0845 6044371
🖷 Fax +44 (0) 1865 312263
🖳 Email myorders@raintreepublishers.co.uk

Customers from outside the UK please telephone +44 1865 312262

Raintree is an imprint of **Capstone Global Library Limited**, a company incorporated in England and Wales having its registered office at 7 Pilgrim Street, London, EC4V 6LB – Registered company number: 6695582

Text © Capstone Global Library Limited 2012
First published in hardback in 2012
First published in paperback in 2013
The moral rights of the proprietor have been asserted.

Edited by Rebecca Rissman and Laura Knowles
Designed by Richard Parker
Picture research by Mica Brancic
Originated by Capstone Global Library Ltd
Printed and bound in China by CTPS

ISBN 978 1 406 23462 6 (hardback)
15 14 13 12 11
10 9 8 7 6 5 4 3 2 1

ISBN 978 1 406 23469 5 (paperback)
16 15 14 13 12
10 9 8 7 6 5 4 3 2 1

British Library Cataloguing in Publication Data
Matthews, Rupert.
World's dumbest dinosaurs. -- (Extreme dinosaurs)
567.9-dc22
A full catalogue record for this book is available from the British Library.

Acknowledgements
We would like to thank the following for permission to reproduce images: © Capstone Publishers pp. **4** (James Field), **5** (James Field), **7** (Steve Weston), **8** (Steve Weston), **8** (Steve Weston), **9** (Steve Weston), **10** (Steve Weston), **11** (Steve Weston), **12** (Steve Weston), **13** (James Field), **14** (Steve Weston), **15** (Steve Weston), **16** (James Field), **17** (James Field), **18** (Steve Weston), **19** (Steve Weston), **21** (Steve Weston), **23** (James Field), **25** (James Field), **27** (James Field); © Miles Kelly Publishing p. **24** (Chris Buzer); Shutterstock p. **29** (© IPK Photography).

Background design features reproduced with permission of Shutterstock/© Szefei/© Fedorov Oleksiy/© Oleg Golovnev/ © Nuttakit.

Cover image of a *Stegosaurus* reproduced with permission of © Capstone Publishers/Steve Weston.

We would like to thank Nathan Smith for his invaluable help in the preparation of this book.

Every effort has been made to contact copyright holders of material reproduced in this book. Any omissions will be rectified in subsequent printings if notice is given to the publishers.

Did you know?
Dinosaurs lived in a
time known as the
Mesozoic Era.

Too dumb to fight

Sauropods like *Apatosaurus* were huge plant-eating **dinosaurs** with long necks and tails. *Apatosaurus* weighed about 27 tonnes. That is as heavy as six elephants!

Despite its huge body size, the brain of *Apatosaurus* was only the size of the brain of a modern cat. With a small brain and big body, *Apatosaurus* may have been really dumb.

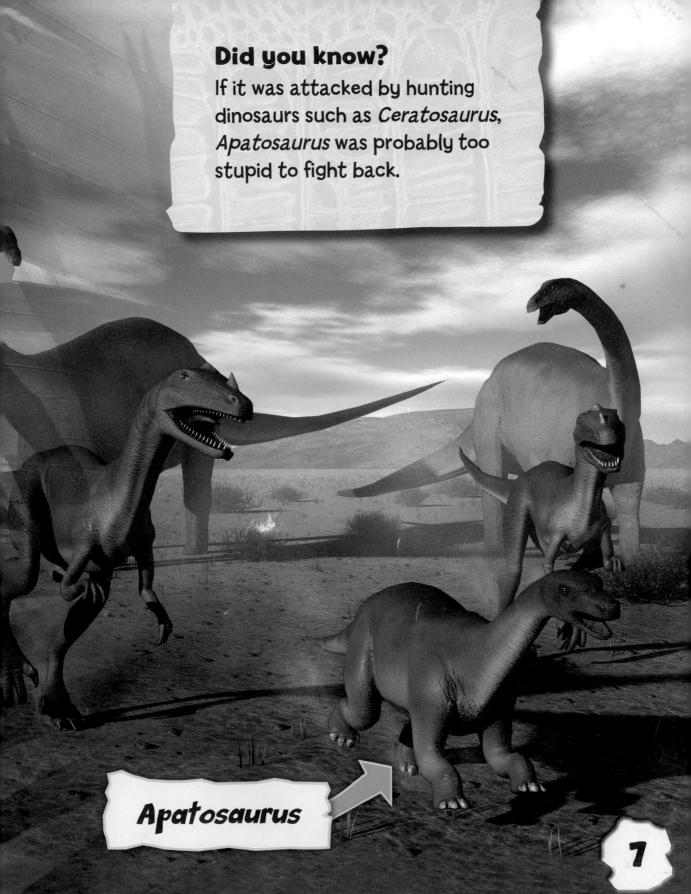

Did you know?
If it was attacked by hunting dinosaurs such as *Ceratosaurus*, *Apatosaurus* was probably too stupid to fight back.

Apatosaurus

The g. eat displa

Argentinosaurus was around 37 metres long and weighed over 100 tonnes. That is about as heavy as 20 elephants. Its brain was no bigger than that of *Apatosaurus*. It must have used most of its brain power to control its big body. It probably had little brain power left over for thinking.

Did you know?
The skeleton of *Argentinosaurus* on display at Fernbank Museum in the United States is the largest **dinosaur** on display anywhere in the world.

Inside the brain

Scientists have found a **fossil** brain of *Tyrannosaurus*. The parts of the brain controlling smell and sight were large, but the thinking part was small. *Tyrannosaurus* probably found **prey** using sight and smell, and then attacked using brute force.

Tyrannosaurus

Armoured stupidity

The **ankylosaurian dinosaur** *Nodosaurus* had **armour** made of bone in bands over its back. Plates of bone armour protected its shoulders, neck, and head. If it was attacked, *Nodosaurus* would lie flat on the ground. This meant that its soft belly was protected. Maybe *Nodosaurus* was not clever enough to think of another way to escape!

Did you know?
Struthiosaurus had spikes of bone as well as armour. It was no cleverer than *Nodosaurus*.

Bonehead

The first **fossil** to be found of the **ankylosaurian** *Panoplosaurus* was a skull found in Alberta, Canada, in 1917. The skull was 0.6 metres long but the brain inside was only about as big as a walnut. Almost all the skull was made up of bone.

Did you know?

Only a few fossil parts of *Panoplosaurus* have been found so scientists view it in different ways. The pictures show two versions of *Panoplosaurus*.

Fruit eater

Pawpawsaurus was an **ankylosaurian** that lived in Texas, USA. The name means "Pawpaw Lizard". Scientists gave it this name because they think it ate soft fruits like pawpaws. *Pawpawsaurus* probably plodded about eating fruits and did not need to think much. It probably had spikes on its shoulders and **armour** all over its back and tail.

Sunbathing

Stegosaurid dinosaurs like *Hesperosaurus* or *Lexovisaurus* had large plates and spikes growing from their backs. Some scientists think these growths protected the stegosaurids from attack. Other scientists think the plates were used to soak up warmth from the Sun. Warm blood means brains can work faster.

Hesperosaurus sunbathing

Lexovisaurus being attacked by two Megalosaurus hunters

A second brain

Stegosaurus was a plant-eating **dinosaur**. Inside its hips was a large space. This space may have held a type of second brain. This would allow the dinosaur to move quickly if it was attacked. However, some scientists think the space was filled by other body **organs**. So the *Stegosaurus* may have been quite dumb after all.

Stegosaurus

Puppy brained

Kentrosaurus could grow to over 4.5 metres long, about the length of a car. Its brain was only about the size of a puppy's brain.

Kentrosaurus might have been unable to think of clever ways to defend itself. If it was attacked, *Kentrosaurus* could face away from its enemy and wave its spiked tail about.

Kentrosaurus

Did you know?
Huayangosaurus was the smallest known **stegosaurid**. Its brain was about as big as an apple.

Brain fever

The tallest **dinosaur** was probably the **sauropod** *Brachiosaurus*, which lived in North America about 150 million years ago. It was about 10.5 metres tall – taller than most houses. Its brain was so small you could hold it in one hand.

Brachiosaurus

Desert walker

Fossils of *Plateosaurus* have been found in rocks that may have since formed into desert. *Plateosaurus* may have walked from one feeding ground to the next.

Plateosaurus fossils have been found in what was mud. Perhaps the **dinosaur** was so stupid it got stuck in mud and could not get out again!

Plateosaurus

Dealing with fossils

Once scientists have found a **dinosaur fossil** they will need to **excavate** it. First the soil and rock on top of the fossil is removed. Next the fossil is removed from the rock in which it has been preserved. The rock may be chipped away with a **chisel**, scratched off with a metal prong (fork), or **dissolved** with acid. The fossil is then wrapped in bubble wrap or cotton wool to be taken to a museum for study.

Glossary

ankylosaurians family of armoured plant-eating dinosaurs that lived between 160 and 65 million years ago

armour outer shell or bone on some dinosaurs that protected their bodies

chisel metal tool with a sharp end

dinosaur group of animals that lived on land millions of years ago during the Mesozoic Era

dissolve melt into a liquid

excavate dig something out of the ground

fossil part of a plant or animal that has been buried in rocks for millions of years

Mesozoic Era part of Earth's history that is sometimes called the "Age of Dinosaurs". It is divided into three periods: Triassic, Jurassic, and Cretaceous.

organs parts of the body such as the heart and lungs

prey animal that is eaten by another animal

sauropod family of plant-eating dinosaurs that had long necks and long tails. The largest dinosaurs of all were sauropods.

stegosaurid group of plant-eating dinosaurs that had spikes or plates of bone sticking out of their backs and tails

Find out more

Books

Dinosaur Encyclopedia, Caroline Bingham
    (Dorling Kindersley, 2009)
Dinosaurs, Stephanie Turnbull (Usborne, 2006)
First Encyclopedia of Dinosaurs and Prehistoric Life,
    Sam Taplin (Usborne, 2011)

Websites

news.bbc.co.uk/cbbcnews/hi/find_out/guides/animals/
    dinosaurs/newsid_1610000/1610405.stm
Learn more about dinosaurs on this BBC website.

www.dinosaurden.co.uk
Information about dinosaurs, as well as puzzles and games
can be found on this site.

www.nhm.ac.uk/kids-only/dinosaurs
The Natural History Museum's website has lots of information
about dinosaurs, including facts, quizzes, and games.

www.thedinosaurmuseum.com/html/dinosaur-facts.html
Find out more about dinosaurs on the Dinosaur Museum website.

Index

ankylosaurians 12–17
Apatosaurus 6–7, 8
Argentinosaurus 8–9
armour 12, 13, 16, 18

bone plates 12, 18
Brachiosaurus 24–25
brains 4, 6, 8, 10, 14, 18, 20,
    22, 23, 24

Canada 14
Ceratosaurus 7

excavate 28

fossils 10, 14, 15, 26, 28

Hesperosaurus 18
Huayangosaurus 23
hunters 7, 10, 19

Kentrosaurus 22

length 8, 22
Lexovisaurus 18, 19

Megalosaurus 19
Mesozoic Era 5

Nodosaurus 12

Panoplosaurus 14–15
Pawpawsaurus 16–17
plant-eaters 6, 16, 20
Plateosaurus 26–27
prey 10

sauropods 6–7, 24–25
sight 10
skeletons 9
skulls 14
smell, sense of 10
spikes 13, 16, 18, 22
stegosaurids 18–19, 23
Stegosaurus 20–21
Struthiosaurus 13
sunbathing 18

Tyrannosaurus 10–11

warm blood 18
weight 6, 8